Zoom In on
Pioneering Explorers

Ferdinand Magellan

Jennifer Strand

abdopublishing.com

Published by Abdo Zoom™, PO Box 398166, Minneapolis, Minnesota 55439. Copyright © 2017 by Abdo Consulting Group, Inc. International copyrights reserved in all countries. No part of this book may be reproduced in any form without written permission from the publisher. Abdo Zoom™ is a trademark and logo of Abdo Consulting Group, Inc.

Printed in the United States of America, North Mankato, Minnesota
072016
092016

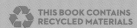
THIS BOOK CONTAINS
RECYCLED MATERIALS

Cover Photo: North Wind Picture Archives
Interior Photos: North Wind Picture Archives, 1, 6, 7, 9, 11, 12, 15, 16, 16–17; DEA/G. Dagli Orti/Getty Images, 5, 19; Photo Researchers, Inc./Science Source, 8; iStockphoto, 10–11; Angela N. Perryman/Shutterstock Images, 13; DEA/M. Seemuller/Getty Images, 14; Houpline-Renard/SIPA/1504201308/AP Images, 18

Editor: Emily Temple
Series Designer: Madeline Berger
Art Direction: Dorothy Toth

Publisher's Cataloging-in-Publication Data
Names: Strand, Jennifer, author.
Title: Ferdinand Magellan / by Jennifer Strand.
Description: Minneapolis, MN : Abdo Zoom, [2017] | Series: Pioneering explorers | Includes bibliographical references and index.
Identifiers: LCCN 2016941515 | ISBN 9781680792416 (lib. bdg.) | ISBN 9781680794090 (ebook) | 9781680794984 (Read-to-me ebook)
Subjects: LCSH: Magalhães, Fernão de, -1521--Travel--Juvenile literature. | Explorers--Portugal--Biography--Juvenile literature. | Voyages around the world--Juvenile literature.
Classification: DDC 910/.92 [B]--dc23
LC record available at http://lccn.loc.gov/2016941515

Table of Contents

Introduction

Ferdinand Magellan was an **explorer**. He led a **voyage** across the Pacific Ocean. No Europeans had sailed across it before.

Early Life

Ferdinand was born in 1480.
He was from Portugal.

His parents died
when he was young.

Ferdinand became a servant for the queen. He studied sailing and mapmaking.

He learned about famous voyages.
Then he became a sailor.

Leader

Magellan went to Asia.
He helped Portugal
trade for spices.

But sailing east to the Spice Islands was hard.

Magellan wanted to sail west.
Portugal's king told him no.

So Magellan went to Spain.
He asked the Spanish king instead.

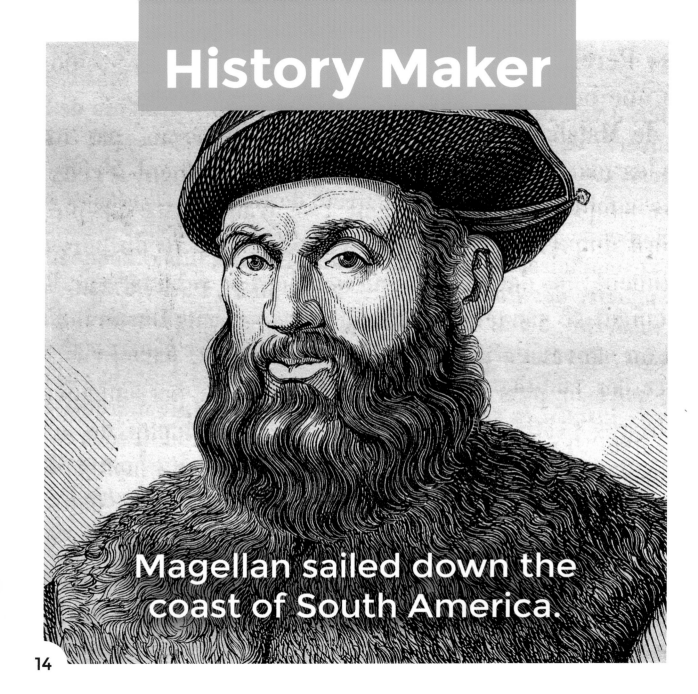

History Maker

Magellan sailed down the coast of South America.

He found a **strait**.
It led to the Pacific Ocean.

His ships sailed west
for more than 90 days.

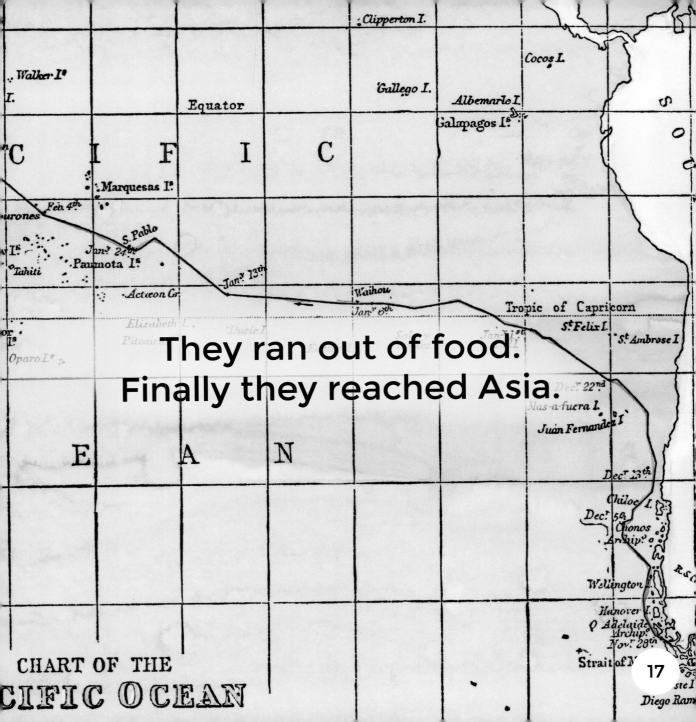

They ran out of food.
Finally they reached Asia.

CHART OF THE
CIFIC OCEAN

Magellan was killed on April 27, 1521. One of his ships kept sailing west.

It was the first ship to sail around the world.

Ferdinand Magellan

Born: 1480

Birthplace: Sabrosa or Porto, Portugal

Wife: Beatriz Barbosa

Known For: Magellan discovered the Strait of Magellan and sailed across the Pacific Ocean. A ship from his voyage sailed around the world.

Died: April 27, 1521

1480: Ferdinand Magellan is born.

1519: Magellan begins his voyage to the Spice Islands.

1520: Magellan finds a strait. It is later called the Strait of Magellan.

1521: Magellan dies on April 27.

1521: Magellan's ships reach the Spice Islands in November.

1522: One of Magellan's ships returns to Spain on September 8. It is the first ship to sail around the world.

Glossary

explorer – a person who travels to new places.

spices – herbs and plants that flavor food.

strait – a narrow waterway that connects two bodies of water.

trade – to give something away in order to get something else in return.

voyage – a long trip to a faraway place.

Booklinks

For more information
on **Ferdinand Magellan**, please visit
booklinks.abdopublishing.com

 **In on Biographies!**

Learn even more with the Abdo Zoom
Biographies database. Check out
abdozoom.com for more information.

Index